I Belong

Parents' Guide

*"I have come that they may have life,
an abundance of life."*

I Belong
First Holy Communion Programme

Published by Redemptorist Publications

Text: Aileen Urquhart
Additional text: Michelle Scott

Illustration and Design: Lis Davis

Copyright © Redemptorist Publications
A Registered Charity Limited by guarantee. Registered in England 3261721

First Published   March 1998
Revised Publication   November 2000
3rd Printing   March 2004

ISBN 0 85231 172 9

Nihil Obstat:
Canon Cyril Murtagh, M.A., S.T.L.
Censor Deputatus

Imprimatur: + Crispian Hollis
Episcopus Portus Magni
Portus Magni December 1997

Printed by Polar Print, Leicester

Redemptorist
PUBLICATIONS
Alphonsus House Chawton Hampshire GU34 3HQ
Telephone 01420 88222   Fax 01420 88805
rp@ShineOnline.net   www.ShineOnline.net

Dear Parent

Welcome to I Belong! Whether this is your first experience of preparation for First Holy Communion or not, you may be interested to know about the thinking behind I Belong.

It seems to me that spirituality, to be valid, has to be grounded in the reality in which we live. This reality is what we see, hear and touch in our daily lives, as well as the overarching reality of "what the eye has not seen, nor ear heard, nor the heart of man conceived" 1 Corinthians 2:9. Genuine spirituality will accept both realities, and find that somehow they are fused (confused seems the wrong word), and we find that the very dirt we walk on is Holy Ground indeed.

Everyday Experience

This programme is therefore very much based on everyday experience, and encourages you and your child to find the deeper realities behind everyday experiences such as eating, working, making up after a row, etc. During each session with you, and then with the children, the catechist explores one of the themes.

The themes are ones that unfold naturally during the celebration of the Eucharist – parenthood, mercy, glory, etc – and extra light is shed on the theme by looking at the Bible. But the themes start and finish with everyday experience. Hopefully the second look at the same experience will be enriched by everything we share about the Eucharist, Church and Bible during the session.

Communication

At this important time for your child and your family it is important to meet together regularly with the catechist(s) and other parents if this is possible. Not only will you receive the practical details that need communicating, but more importantly you have a wonderful opportunity to get to grips with the theme by hearing other people's insights and difficulties. The questions and reflections you and your child experience will almost certainly be what is on the minds of other parents and children. If you do not know many people in your parish, you now have a wonderful chance to get to know the First Communion families really well. The community aspect of the Eucharist is much more obvious when you are in a distinct community already.

The beauty of basing the sessions on personal experience is that there are no right or wrong answers. If someone says he has never experienced the glory of God's presence, this is a valid comment. If someone says she gasps in wonder every time she sees a rainbow, this is valid also. In this instance the task of the catechist is to reach, and enable the group to reach, a greater understanding of the glory of God. Listening to one another, to what the Bible says, what the Church says, listening to the Spirit stirring within us, will bring about understanding: an understanding of the heart more than of the intellect.

Your own spiritual life

Of course, knowledge is necessary, and it is important to know what the Bible and the Church are saying to us. Reading the Bible prayerfully is very important. The documents of Vatican II and the New Catechism are very enlightening as to what the Church is saying. A useful additional resource is the General Directory for Catechesis. You probably have your own selection of good spiritual writers that inspire you.

Above all, it is important to PRAY. If you are busy, and most people are these days, it is easy to put off any serious attempt at prayer, and just get by with a few quick words and a promise to "do better tomorrow" I find that tomorrow is just as busy as today, and my life is a series of promises to God. However I still believe that prayer is the most important thing you can do. I am going to stop making promises to God, and actually spend some "quality" time praying now!

I hope you enjoy using 'I Belong. I hope it helps you, the team, parents and children, to grow in the love of Jesus, present in the bread and wine, present in one another. After all, this is what is at the heart of our faith, isn't it?

God bless your work.

Aileen B. Urquhart

Aileen B. Urquhart

Contents

Introduction

I Belong is a preparation journey which is based on the framework of our celebration of the Eucharist. All the material is firmly grounded in the Bible and in the Catechism of the Catholic Church, and full references are given for your preparation of each section.

1. **In the Name of the Father**   Introductory Rites

2. **Lord have Mercy**

3. **Celebrating our Rescue** (reconciliation)

4. **God Helps Me Get it Right** (reconciliation)

5. **Glory to God in the Highest**

6. **This is the Word of the Lord**   Liturgy of the Word

7. **Bread to Offer**   Liturgy of the Eucharist

8. **Fruit of the Vine**

9. **Do this in Memory of Me**

10. **Body of Christ**

11. **To Love and to Serve**   Concluding Rites

I Belong includes two sections on reconciliation which are complementary to any First Reconciliation programme your children follow. Alternatively, the first sections of I Belong can be adapted and developed as a separate preparation for First Reconciliation

"I have come that they may have life, an abundance of life."

Each session the children will be exploring a theme connected with the Eucharist (Mass). They will start by looking at their ordinary experiences of the theme — beginning with **Names** and **Parents** — and then go on to think about the theme in Scripture, and in Church. Finally, they will look again at everyday experiences, and hopefully discover how the Eucharist is about **REAL LIFE**.

SESSION 1 IN THE NAME OF THE FATHER

Your child's preparation for First Holy Communion begins with this first session which focuses on names. We will also be talking about baptism.

Page 3 Everyday Life

The names we are called can affect us deeply. You probably spent a long time choosing a name for your child. It had to be just right. You may also remember suffering as a child if you were constantly called names such as lazy-bones, or heard your parents label you in some way or another.

Pages 4 to 7 Scripture

In scripture, the use of names is often very significant. Adam (the name means 'of the earth') represents all of us, men and women alike. The link with earth is not to be despised. Creation is glorious. Genesis tells us that God saw creation was good … good … very good. Adam's naming of animals means that we have power, and therefore responsibility, over the rest of creation.

At the Annunciation God became part of this glorious creation, thus making it even more magnificent. By becoming human, God became subject to other human beings, and was also *named.* The name Jesus (Joshua) means *saviour.* In the *Old Testament*, Joshua was one who led the Israelites over the River Jordan into the freedom of the Promised Land after their forty years in the desert. It was not by accident that Jesus was baptised in the Jordan. He is the true Joshua, leading us all to fulfilment and life.

The baptism of Jesus also has links with the story of creation. Just as in *Genesis* the Spirit of God hovered over the waters of chaos and brought forth life, so the Spirit hovered over Jesus. Jesus is the *second Adam* – the new creation. In Adam, we walk in friendship with God. In Jesus, we are re-created as children of God.

Page 8 Picture to colour in

Page 9 Church

For Jesus, his baptism was a powerful sign of his sonship. He experienced God as *Father*, and this experience was to colour everything he said and did. In baptism, we are saying many things. We are not only celebrating the new life – the new *Adam* – that has been brought into the world, but also joining Jesus in his *Abba-experience*. Baptism is the Spirit breathing life into the chaos, it is the crossing over the waters of Jordan into a new life of liberty, it is God calling us to be his beloved children.

It is our baptism that gives us the right to come together as Church. It unites us all as children of God – all equal – all loved.

Page 10 Everyday Life

It would be wonderful to be constantly aware of our dignity as children of God. So often we put ourselves down. *"Oh I'm so stupid," "Oh you are a nuisance."* Perhaps we could start saying nice things about ourselves and others. We are all God's beloved children.

At home you might like to go through the *Our Father* with your child, explaining some of the more difficult words. If you don't say night prayers together this could be a good time to start. You could also talk about his/her baptism. If you had a party at the time, tell your child about it. Much of the scripture that we will be looking at during the next few months will mention parties and celebrations, and refer to the celebration of your child's **First Holy Communion**.

Encourage your child to use their book.

LORD HAVE MERCY

This session the children will be thinking about mercy in everyday life, scripture, and church. Hopefully they will come to a better understanding of the mercy of God, and how we are called to be merciful in our day to day dealings with people. At the Eucharist we come before our loving God to receive infinite mercy, and are challenged and empowered to pass on this gift freely.

Page 14 Everyday life

Children are completely dependent on the merciful love of adults. Their concept of mercy will depend on the experience of mercy that they receive from **us**. God is traditionally portrayed as a father. The idea of God will be based on the parenting they receive from **us**. If we forgive them willingly, and forget past bad behaviour, they will grow up with confidence in life, and in the God who gave us life.

Page 16 Old Testament

The creation stories in the Bible were written in about 1000 B.C. King David had united the tribes into one kingdom and there was relative peace and prosperity. People had time to think about the meaning of life, and other big questions such as the problem of suffering and evil. Under the inspiration of God *Genesis* was written. What it contains is not *scientific truth* but *theological* truth. The story of the serpent and the forbidden fruit acknowledges that although wonderfully created, we all struggle with the temptation towards evil. However, this basic weakness of ours shows God's wonderful mercy towards us, in the promise of a Saviour. Every year during the Easter Vigil we hear the sin of Adam called a *"happy fault"*.

Page 17 New Testament

We will be looking closely at the story of the Forgiving Father at the parents' sessions. There is a bit of each character in the story in all of us. We can in turn be the forgiving father, the tearaway younger son and the self-righteous elder brother. A good book on this is *The Return of the Prodigal Son* by Henri Nouwen.

Page 19 Picture to colour in

Page 20 Church

We say *Lord Have Mercy – Kyrie Eleison* at the Eucharist. Some scholars say the word eleison comes from the word for olive. The *mercy* we receive from God is like the olive twig symbol of hope, that the dove brought to Noah when the flood waters subsided. We can imagine the Prodigal Son being freshly bathed and anointed with oil of the olives before he put on the new robes, sandals and ring. We are reminded of the anointing of priests and kings in the Bible, and of our own anointing as holy and royal people at our baptism. This rich abundance is what we expect from God when we ask for *mercy*.

Read *School for Prayer* by *Archbishop Anthony Bloom* for more about this.

Page 21 Everyday life

There is a playground game called *"Mercy, Mercy"* in which one child squeezes another child's finger until the other cries for mercy. This is not what we mean by mercy. We mean something altogether more positive, more like an aromatherapy massage. Shakespeare puts it like this:

"The quality of mercy is not strained; It droppeth as the gentle rain from heaven upon the place beneath. It is twice blest: it blesseth him that gives and him that takes.
'Tis mightiest in the mightiest; it becomes the throned monarch better than his crown;...
It is enthroned in the hearts of kings,
It is an attribute of God himself..."
Merchant of Venice, Act IV

CELEBRATING OUR RESCUE

This is the first of two sessions to help the children pre-pare for their First Reconciliation. At the next session they will be thinking about how God helps them 'get it right' and how Reconciliation can give us help for the future. To begin with though, they will be thinking of how we are always being rescued by God. Reconciliation is always taking place in everyday life, and the Sacrament of Reconciliation is an opportunity to praise God for his understanding, help and forgiveness in the past.

Page 25 Everyday life

You could remind your child of any rescue they have seen. Maybe a road accident or fire. Perhaps they tried to rescue a bird fallen out of a tree, or stood up for a younger child when they were being bullied. If your child has ever been lost, you could discuss how they felt. (The odds are **YOU** were even more worried than they were!) Use this as an illustration of how pleased God is when we are back on the right path.

What we need to get across to the children is that **they are basically GOOD, and that sometimes they lose their way and need "rescuing",** not that they are sinful and need constant correcting, in order that they will occasionally be good and lovable.

Page 27 Old Testament

In the past, our picture of God has sometimes been distorted. Because people have seen God as all-holy, perfect, etc. they have stressed the distance between God and human beings, and dwelt on our sinfulness and unworthiness. We need to get back to the image of God as a loving parent, and see ourselves as made in the image and likeness of God. As we have said, God is Emmanuel – God with us *"Can a mother forget her child? Even if she did, I would not forget you."* (Isaiah 49:15)

Page 28 New Testament

The Parable of the Lost Sheep is one of three parables – (the Lost Sheep, the Lost Coin, the Prodigal Son) all together in Luke's Gospel – about God's joy over returning sinners. They are three stories told to the self-righteous scribes and Pharisees who were disgusted at Jesus because he mixed with "publicans and sinners". In Jewish law, certain occupations automatically made people sinners, as you were unable to keep the outward observances of the law.

Page 29 Picture to colour

Pages 30 Everyday Life again

The children will be thinking about feelings, and how they are useful signals to their needs. At home you are good shepherds to your children when you empathise with their anger, hurt, envy, etc. and rescue them by helping them find good ways of dealing with their problems. **NEVER SAY TO YOUR CHILD 'I WON'T LOVE/LIKE YOU IF...'** Apart from being a devastating statement, it is not a true reflection of God's parenthood. **GOD IS LOVE**.

Page 31 Church

Because Catholics have often inherited this tendency to stress the distance between God and us, reconciliation is seen as something very negative. Try to stress the **celebration** aspect with your child. We are celebrating God's forgiving love and on-going help. A modern definition of a sacrament is *"a festive action in which Christians assemble to celebrate their lived experience and to call to heart their common story. The action is a symbol of God's care for us in Christ. Enacting the symbol brings us closer to one another in the church, and to the Lord who is there for us."*

Tad Guzie. The Book of Sacramental Basics.

SESSION 4 GOD HELPS ME GET IT RIGHT
RECONCILIATION

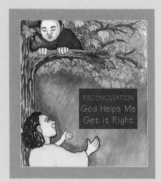

At our last session we thought about how God rescues us from past failings, and how reconciliation is going on in life all the time. We go to Reconciliation to CELEBRATE God's forgiving love. When we CONFIDE in the priest we are CONFIDENT that the sacrament gives us help for the times we "get it wrong". This session we are still thinking about celebrating, but with a focus on the future.

Page 37 Everyday life

Remind the children about achievements like learning to swim, ride a bike, read a book. A lot of mistakes went into each process, but you were there to encourage and help. It is probably your experience that any time you were impatient or uninterested in their struggles they did not do very well, and even shrivelled up a bit, but when you gave your whole-hearted attention to their struggle they seemed to blossom. God is the good parent, who encourages us even when we fail. God's belief in us gives us the courage to believe in ourselves. God says, *"Go on, I know you can do it"*, and we find it is true.

Page 39-40 New Testament

The children have had two parables about forgiveness already – The Prodigal Son and the Lost Sheep. Each story ends with a party – a celebration that what was lost is now found. They are now hearing about a real-life situation when Jesus **"practises what he preaches"**. Jesus searches out the lost son of Abraham and the celebration itself brings about the wonderful transformation in Zacchaeus.

Zacchaeus, the tax collector, was a collaborator with the Roman authorities, so was considered a traitor by the 'decent' people. Tax collectors collected the money that the Romans exacted, but they were allowed to collect any amount they liked and they pocketed the difference. It was this man whom Jesus singled out to dine with. The effect on Zacchaeus was remarkable. Having been affirmed by Jesus, he confessed his guilt and decided to make amends. His offer to pay back four times what he had wrongly taken was a direct reference to the Jewish law – he was acting as a good Jew now not as a public sinner, for as Jesus said of him, *"This man too is a son of Abraham."* The message for us is – **if we treat our children as sons and daughters of God they will act like sons and daughters of God.**

Page 41 Picture to colour in

Pages 42 to 44 The Sacrament

These pages have a lot of reading for the children, and in their sessions with the catechists they will not have time to discuss all the points. Please go through them with your child, so they are quite confident as to what Reconciliation is all about. You will notice that the emphasis is very positive. We are thanking God for his forgiveness, and asking help for the future. God really does believe in us (we are made in God's image after all!) and says to us, as Jesus said to the woman taken in adultery, *"Go, and sin no more"*.

Finally — enjoy your child's First Reconciliation. It is a celebration, just as Baptism, Confirmation, First Communion, Marriage, Ordination, and even the Sacrament of the Sick are celebrations.

SESSION 5 GLORY TO GOD IN THE HIGHEST

This session the children will be thinking about glory. This is a difficult concept, but a very important one. Everything Jesus did was for the GLORY of his Father, and to follow in his footsteps all our actions should also be for the honour and glory of God.

Page 49 Everyday Life

The children may not have had many experiences of actually receiving GLORY, but they may well have had experiences which leave them gasping with wonder. A magnificent fireworks display, or the first time they see snow are two possibilities among thousands.

Page 51 Old Testament

The **GLORY** *(shekinah)* of God is spoken of again and again in the Old Testament. In the burning bush episode we learn that we cannot name God *(I Am who I Am)* for God is beyond us.

However we learn that this **HOLY GOD** is a God who **SAVES**. God led the slaves through the desert to freedom, the *shekinah* remaining with them as a pillar of fire by night, and of cloud by day.

Page 52 New Testament

Just as Moses the shepherd saw the **GLORY** of the Lord on the mountain, so did the shepherds of Bethlehem see the **GLORY** on the hills of Bethlehem. Just like Moses, they were afraid, and yet once again there is a message of deliverance from God. Shepherds were *outside the law* as far as respectable people were concerned. They were unable to keep the strict laws of washing which the Pharisees had imposed on the people, and so were imprisoned in a *"sinful"* condition. Once again God approaches people caught up in slavery, and gives them the Good News of peace. God is with us — Emmanuel.

Page 54 Picture to Colour in

Page 55 Church

The whole of the Eucharist is a prayer of praise and thanks to the **GLORY** of God. (*The word Eucharist means thank you. In Greece today you can still hear people saying efcharisto – thank you.*)

At the Eucharist the children could listen out for how many times the word **GLORY**, and similar words are mentioned. In their session they will be thinking about the **GLORIA**, but there are other important prayers of praise. The words of the Preface change, according to what aspect of God's glory we are praising and being thankful for. There is also the beautiful prayer,

Through him, with him, and in him,
in the unity of the Holy Spirit,
all glory and honour is yours,
almighty Father,
for ever and ever.

The response of AMEN is everyone's chance to make the prayer their own. The sound should bring the roof down! The children could be encouraged to really shout it out!

When the shepherds left the magnificent glory of God on the hillside, they arrived at the quiet glory of a baby in a manger. At the Eucharist we meet the quiet glory of God in the bread and wine. The more we are aware of the wonder of the **REAL PRESENCE** the more will our children appreciate this breath-taking **MYSTERY OF FAITH**.

56 Everyday life

St Irenaeus said *"The glory of God is a human being fully alive"*. This is seen most powerfully in Jesus, but the glory of God is also shining in each one of us. We and our children are burning bushes. When we approach one another we approach Holy Ground. Let us teach our children to reverence the holiness of others. To love God and to love our neighbour are two sides of the same coin.

SESSION 6 THIS IS THE WORD OF THE LORD

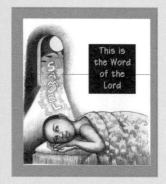

In this session the children will be thinking about listening to the Word of God. The first half of the Eucharist is called the Liturgy of the Word, and what we listen to focuses our minds on a particular reason for glorifying God, depending on the season of the Church's year, the feast, etc.

Page 61 Everyday life

The children have a "fun" start this session, thinking about how animals would survive without ears! They will then think about how well they themselves would survive if they didn't **LISTEN**. (The catechists are aware that some children may have hearing problems, and will be sensitive to this.) The idea is to help them consider how listening to the Word of the Lord helps us to live in confidence as children of God.

Page 63 Old Testament

The children read the story of Samuel in the temple. Hannah had wept and prayed for a child, and promised him to the Lord if she should have one. When Samuel was born, Hannah sang a song of praise to God, recounting the marvellous saving works of God in lifting up the poor and feeding the hungry. Years later, Mary would use this song as a basis for her song of praise to God, when her cousin Elizabeth acknowledged the presence of the Saviour in Mary's womb. This prayer, known as the **Magnificat**, is still used every evening in the *Prayer of the Church (Divine Office)*.

The children will concentrate on the story of Samuel hearing God call him in the night. The children are like Samuel (and Jesus) in that they are gifts from God. Baptism not only marks their entry into the community, but also makes them **"prophets"** who hear God's word and carry it out to others, just as Samuel (and, of course, Jesus) did. Holy Communion will mark their entry into full membership of the community and as well as making them holy, will give them strength to be prophets: pro-God and pro-others.

Page 65 New Testament

In the Old Testament, there were many prophets who brought God's word to the people. Jesus is more than the greatest of the prophets – he **IS** God's Word. Jesus is the *embodiment* of God. God responds to our poverty and need by becoming poor and needy. God is indeed *Emmanuel — "God with us"*.

The word *"Bethlehem"* means "House of Bread". In Jesus the songs of Hannah and Mary are fulfilled, for in him God comes to our rescue – the poor and hungry are fed.

The promise is kept today in the Eucharist when God is with us as the Bread of Life, and we go out from the Eucharist with a mission to feed the hungry – to be saviours ourselves to those in need.

Page 66 Picture to colour in

Page 67 Church

The readings at the Eucharist are often above the heads of the children and they can be bored. If your parish has a children's Eucharist on Sundays the children will have their own special Liturgy of the Word, when they listen and think about the Readings at their own level of understanding. Another way to focus their minds on the Eucharist is to take one word — e.g. *glory* or *Father* and listen out for it during the Eucharist. This can be helpful for adults as well.

Page 68 Everyday Life

The children are finishing with a Snakes and Ladders type game, where they go up a Ladder if they listen to good/nice things, and down a Snake if they don't listen (or listen to bad ideas!) Please play it at home with your children. It is giving them the message that what we listen to affects us.

SESSION 7 BREAD TO OFFER

Until now the children were thinking about the first part of the Eucharist — the Liturgy of the Word. They are now turning to the second part — the Liturgy of the Eucharist. In this session the children will be thinking about the Preparation of the Gifts/Offertory.

Page 73 Everyday Life

You will have more time than the catechists to discuss with your child all that has to happen before a meal can take place. You could think about some of the products you eat, the danger the fishermen undergo, the length of time the farmer has to care for his crop, etc. Perhaps you could work out how many hours' work the food on your table costs!

Page 75 Old Testament

The people in the desert were entirely at the mercy of God (and the heat, lack of food and water etc.) In their wanderings they learnt to trust that God would provide, and developed a real understanding of what *"bread"* stands for. To a large extent we have lost this understanding, and maybe even lost a realisation of how dependent we are on God. When hardships hit us we can either grumble, like the Israelites did at first, or develop an attitude of trust in God, who **"gives us our daily bread"**.

The Israelites were instructed to gather only enough for their daily needs. If they gathered too much the manna putrefied. However the day before the Sabbath they were instructed to gather twice as much so they could rest on the Sabbath. This amount did not putrefy and they were able to eat on the day of rest. Throughout their journey the Israelites were fed on the manna, rather like we, the new People of God, are fed on the bread of life throughout our life's journey.   (*Exodus 16*)

Page 77 New Testament

Three of the gospels, Matthew, Mark and Luke, give accounts of the Last Supper of Jesus. John does not. Instead, he puts his teaching about the Eucharist in Chapter 6, the Feeding of the Five Thousand. The children will be thinking about the little boy who offered up his five loaves and two fishes. Jesus took these, and enabled his disciples to feed the crowd, with twelve baskets of scraps left over. As adults, we can go deeper into the mystery, and read all that Jesus said about himself after this great **sign**. One thing worth mentioning is that Jesus said, *"I am the Bread of Life."* He makes seven "I AM" statements in John's gospel. You may remember that when Moses asked God's name he was told **"I AM WHO I AM."** Jesus is telling us that he, God, the great I AM, is feeding us with his own self, and we shall live forever.

Page 78 Picture to colour in

Page 79 Church

As said earlier, we are probably out of touch with the deep significance of presenting bread to God. We are so dependent on food that we are offering God our very existence. To put it less grandly, when we offer up the bread it stands for all the sweat and labour, the tedium of the past week – everything we do to keep a roof above our heads and the wolf from the door. The offering of the money is also deeply significant. It is not an interruption of the Eucharist, but very much part of it. At the beginning of the Bible, in Genesis 14, Melchisedech, the king of Salem and Priest of God Most High, offered bread and wine to God, and Abram (later called Abraham) gave him a tenth of all his wealth.

We will think about the wine next time.

Page 80 Everyday Life

Just as the disciples fed the crowds with the bread, we go out to others to feed the world. Our gratitude to God opens up a spirit of generosity in us, and the Eucharist not only feeds us but empowers us to go out to others.

SESSION 8   <u>FRUIT OF THE VINE</u>

In this session the children will be thinking about the wine as we use it at the Eucharist, and why we use it. As adults we can understand that wine not only symbolises celebration, but that it also stands for sorrow — we talk of a cup of sorrow. If we share a cup with someone we are intimately connected with them. We share their destiny. Although the children will touch on the sorrowful aspect, they will be concentrating on the joy of celebrations.

Page 85 Everyday Life

Often children don't like the taste of wine, so on their first page they will be thinking about tastes they didn't like when they were younger, but do like now. This links in with the idea of **sacrifice** in the wine. They had to give up the comfort of a bottle in order to appreciate other drinks/food. Hopefully it will also prepare them for the practicalities of drinking wine at the First Eucharist and afterwards. At home you might like them to taste wine if they haven't yet done so. Communion wine is usually sweet and rich.

Page 87 Old Testament

The Passover feast was held every spring to celebrate the deliverance from slavery of the People of God. The feast was not just held in memory of the past. To the Jews, celebrating this feast makes God's saving action present and available to them in the here and now.

The People of God thought of themselves as the vineyard of God. Other references to themselves as God's vineyard are in Psalm 80 – *"You have brought a grapevine out of Egypt … Turn to us Almighty God … Come and save this grapevine that you planted."*

Page 89 New Testament

The children will think about the celebration that Jesus provided at the wedding feast at Cana. So many gallons of wine is really lavish – rather like the miracle of the loaves and fishes when twelve baskets were left over! The abundance of wine is a symbol that the fullness of the Kingdom has arrived (Isaiah 25:6). As adults, we can read more into the miracle (sign). It was *"on the third day"* which links with the Resurrection. Jesus took the water (standing for the old ritualism of the original Covenant) and changed it into wine, standing for the wine of the New Covenant.

Page 91 Picture to colour in

Page 92 The Church

The link between the Jewish Passover and the Eucharist is very obvious in the Passover prayer (on page 87 in the children's book). The Eucharist is very much a Thank You prayer for all the good things of creation.

We also think of ourselves as a vine. Jesus said he was the vine and we are the branches. He is not separate from us – a vine IS the branches – we are the New Risen Body of Christ. *"Whatever you do to the least one of these, you do it to me,"* said Jesus.

Just as the Passover makes God's action present for the Jews, so the Eucharist makes God's action present for us. We are liberated from slavery to sin by receiving the life of Christ. We not only look to the past, to Christ's redeeming acts of death and resurrection, but also to the future. At the Last Supper Jesus said he would not drink again till he drank the new wine of the Kingdom of God. At the Eucharist we bring about the Wedding Feast of the Lamb, and God eats with the New People of God.

Page 93 Everyday Life

The Kingdom of God will not come about unless we take the Eucharist seriously. Properly understood, the Eucharist means that we join with Jesus in bringing the Good News to the world no matter what the cost.

In the Eucharist we are uniting ourselves to the selfless love of Jesus in giving up his life for his friends. *"No one has greater love than he who gives up his life for his friends."* (John 15:13) This is exactly what Jesus did.

SESSION 9 DO THIS IN MEMORY OF ME

We now come to the heart of the Eucharist — the "Institution Narrative". At this part of the Eucharist the Holy Spirit is invoked: "Let your Spirit come upon these gifts," and the Words of Consecration are said. Jesus is made present on the altar in a new way. His presence remains in the consecrated hosts reserved in the tabernacle on the altar. The word tabernacle comes from the tent of meeting in the desert (Exodus 25:8). Jesus is already present as God, in Scripture, in the priest and people, and other ways, but this new presence is so special it is called the Real Presence. In this sacrament Jesus is present in a unique way, whole and entire, God and man, substantially and permanently.

Page 99 Everyday Life

We have meals for all sorts of reasons – for comfort, because we are hungry, to sustain us, to celebrate, to sit down and relax etc. Meals can be quick snacks in railway cafes, where we pay more attention to our luggage than the food and company, a great banquet in honour of someone special, an impromptu barbecue when friends call or a relaxing gathering of the family.

Some meals really change us in some way. Sharing the same food and conversation can bring us closer together, and we gain new insights into each other and into the topics of conversation.

Page 101 Old Testament

There is only one page on the Old Testament in this session, as we are concentrating more on the Last Supper, and we have talked about the Passover before. However it might be worth noting that the word Passover comes from the fact that the Israelites sacrificed a lamb, and put the blood on their door-posts so that God **"passed over"** their houses. Because of the blood of the lamb the Israelites did not suffer the tenth plague – the death of the eldest son. (We are not covering this with the children).

Page 102 New Testament

Jesus took an existing feast, the most important of the Jewish celebrations, and changed it into something new. Throughout the Old Testament, God is constantly renewing the Covenant made with human beings. In the Book of Jeremiah, God promises a New Covenant, not like the previous one. In the New Covenant, *"I will put my law within them. I will write it upon their hearts. I will be their God and they shall be my people …*

they shall all know me, from the least of them to the greatest. I will forgive them and forget their sins." (Jeremiah 31:31-34)

Jesus brought about this New Covenant at his Last Supper when he, the new Lamb of God, offered his life, present in the bread and in the Cup of Salvation (*the Blood of the New and Everlasting Covenant*).

Once again, we are not mentioning 'blood' to the children, although we are talking about Jesus dying for us. In Western cultures, we usually associate *blood* with *death*; for the Jews, *blood* meant *life*.

Page 104 Picture to colour in

Page 105 Church

At the Eucharist, help your child listen out for the words of Consecration, and the Lamb of God. Don't try to go into long explanations of how Christ is present if they ask **HOW**. Just remember that the presence isn't that of a physical body. (In the next session we will look at how, after the Resurrection, Jesus' body was so transformed he could pass through locked doors and his friends didn't recognise him!) The mystery of Christ present in the Eucharist is so amazing it is called **THE MYSTERY OF FAITH**.

Page 106 Everyday Life

Enjoy your meals together. Make them life-giving occasions!

SESSION 10 BODY OF CHRIST

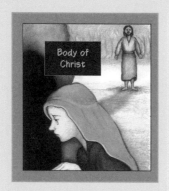

This session we are looking at the words the priest says as he distributes the host and the cup — "The Body of Christ" and "The Blood of Christ". We are thinking about HOW Christ is present in the bread and wine.

Page 111 Everyday Life

The children will be thinking about how tadpoles and caterpillars change into frogs and butterflies. The outer appearances change, but the inner reality is the same. They will be led to think about how the opposite happens at the Eucharist. At Mass the outer appearances of the bread and wine are the same, but the inner reality is different.

Old Testament

There is no Old Testament story this session in order to have two New Testament stories. The Old Testament stories have been leading up to this fulfilment of God's promise in the New Covenant.

Pages 113 and 116 New Testament

The two stories (Christ appearing to Mary Magdalen, and to the friends on the way to Emmaus) have been chosen to illustrate the fact that he looked different. He had a different kind of body. At home you could remind your children of Christ's appearances in the Upper Room, first when Thomas was absent, then when he was there. Christ's body could go through locked doors, but he wasn't a ghost – he ate with them, and Thomas could touch him. After the Resurrection Jesus could appear as a gardener, a stranger, he could come and go suddenly and mysteriously. He was not limited by the normal constraints of human life. And yet, it was the same Jesus whom they knew and loved. At Emmaus, the friends recognised him in the *"breaking of the bread"* – in the Eucharist.

Page 115 Picture to colour in

Page 117 Church

It is in the Eucharist that we recognise him too. We look at the outward appearances of bread and wine, but recognise Jesus in the **"breaking of the bread"**. Don't try to go into long explanations of how Christ is present. It is such a unique mystery it is called **THE Mystery of Faith**. Technical explanations might take away the wonder of it all, rather like explaining how rainbows occur at the very moment the child has been surprised by one. The introduction about tadpoles and caterpillars is more about the wonder of the changes that they can see, to prepare them for the wonder of the change that they can't see.

Page 118 Everyday life

There is so much to say, and so little time! When we go to the Eucharist sometimes we feel wonderful, sometimes we feel hypocritical, sometimes we feel we have the strength to conquer the world afterwards, sometimes we go back to old bad habits. The truth of it is that we are a wounded people just as Jesus was wounded. If we could try to look at one another in the community and indeed in the world, and see this new Body of Christ, and love one another with the compassion of Christ, the Eucharist will have borne fruit. There will be more about this aspect of the Eucharist in the next session, but for this one, in the last week or so before your child's communion, encourage them to pray quietly to Jesus, and pray together as a family if you feel you can do so. Bearing in mind that they may not feel anything very much after their First Holy Communion (there's a lot of practicalities for them to think about, and they might be nervous), tell them that the time after receiving the Eucharist is a very special time, both for them and Jesus. Time spent in stillness and reverence will help them. *"recognise him in the breaking of the bread.'*

SESSION 11 TO LOVE AND TO SERVE

Our last session of the programme! This will be a shorter session than the earlier ones to allow time for a party at the end. Please encourage your child to finish their book at home. We will be concentrating on getting the children to write a "thank you letter" to their Prayer Sponsors. Some of you may have already asked your children to do this. Your child will also be given the name of a new child for them to pray for next year.

Page 123 Everyday Life

At meal times you could make the link between everyday food and spiritual food. Communion gives us strength for living as Christians. If we don't eat of this food regularly we are (literally) not in communion with the Body of Christ. The Eucharist is called the **"source and summit"** of the People of God.

If you don't normally thank God for your food at meal times you might like to introduce this, and add a prayer for those who haven't enough to eat.

Page 125 Old Testament

There won't be enough time to remind the children of the whole story of humanity as seen through the eyes of the Jewish people. You could go back over the whole book (or better still, a children's Bible) and trace the story from Adam and Eve to the entry into the Promised Land. When the people were in the Promised Land they had time to work out their laws, traditions, feasts, etc. In fact it was only after they settled down that they wrote down the stories of Adam and Eve, Abraham, etc.

Page 126 New Testament

This story, like the one of Emmaus last session, is a **"model"** of the Eucharist. Christ feeds us and asks us to do likewise: *"Feed my lambs and sheep"*. Note that the apostles, including trained fishermen, couldn't catch fish themselves. There are many other stories you could tell your children about how we bring about the Kingdom of God (how we enter the Promised Land). For example: *"I was hungry and you gave me food"* is a good one. *Matthew 25:34-40*

Page 128 Picture to colour in

Page 129 Church

Sometimes people say they don't need to go to church as they are just as good as church-goers, or even that church-goers are hypocrites. This may be true, as we are a Church of sinners, but the Eucharist, properly understood, strengthens us to serve others. What we put into it, and what we receive from it has a direct bearing on how we live every day.

Your child has prepared for the Eucharist, and received Holy Communion. The catechists hope that the children, and you, have all enjoyed the Course. There is so much to learn, and we will never understand the glory of the Eucharist in this life. However, we cannot know God by the intellect. It is the heart that understands and loves.

May God bless you and your family.

Dear Grandparent,

You are reading this because your grandchild is preparing for his/her First Holy Communion. You may be a silver-haired old grandad, a glamourous young granny, or somebody quite different. You may be a devout churchgoer, an atheist, or something in between these two. But whoever or whatever you are, your grandchild is taking an important step in preparing for First Holy Communion, and your loving involvement can enrich the whole process.

Your grandchild's first steps

A child's first steps are very precious. You can probably remember when your own child was learning to walk, and if you were lucky you were there when your grandchild began to toddle. You had to decide how much help to give, and when to let go. There were many tumbles, but with some tears, and much laughter the infant began to walk. You may have had mixed feelings as your child grew from dependency to independence.

You may also have mixed feelings as your grandchild takes the step of preparing for First Holy Communion. It will depend on your relationship with the Catholic Church You may be delighted, dubious or aghast at the idea! If your feelings are different to that of the child's parent(s) this could be a complication, and you will need to use the wisdom and diplomacy that come with maturity.

Freedom of choice

If your journey towards wholeness and fulfilment follows a different path from your grandchild, please remember that – with his parent(s) – he/she has decided to walk in full communion with the Catholic Church, and to be nourished in that journey by Jesus, the bread of life. No matter how painful this may be, please respect his freedom to choose, and take an interest in your grandchild's preparation. If you feel badly towards the Catholic Church, you may find that a closer look gives you a pleasant surprise.

Perhaps you are a fully committed Catholic, and have had to do a lot of running around to ensure that your grandchild is brought up as a Catholic because your own child does not go to church often. If you are reading this letter, you have probably succeeded in getting your grandchild enrolled in preparation sessions, but tact will be necessary here also. Just as you can't force a baby to walk before he is ready, so you can't force a child to love God in the way you do. You need the wisdom to know when to encourage and when to stand back. Pray for your grandchild and his/her family. Keep up to date with Church teaching so that you can answer questions if necessary.

New insights

If you are a regular church-going Catholic, and so is your family, you are in a happy position. Not only can your faith be a shining example to everyone, you will probably find that your grandchild will give you new insights into the Eucharist. Children have an uncanny knack of asking very searching questions. You may find that as you search for answers, your relationship with Christ takes on a new lease of life you didn't think was possible.

The following thoughts may help you understand more fully the important step your grandchild is taking, and how closely you are involved.

- Love cannot contain itself and one of the fruits of your love for your partner was your child. Just as Jesus said to those he loved at the Last Supper, you said to your partner, " **This is my body, given for you"**. This giving was not a one-off thing, but a way of life. Now you can look back and see how, in the good times and the bad times, your body has been given, your life's blood has been poured out for those you love. Your giving of your life was, literally, life-giving.

- Your body may not be all that it once was! Like Jesus, you bear the marks of love, of daily sacrifice for your family. But like Jesus, you live to see the fruits of that love – the love that will not contain itself, but is reborn in your children and your children's children.

In the next few months your grandchild is going to reflect more and more on the life-giving love God gives us in Jesus, and which is shown most clearly in the Eucharist, the Sacrament of Love. Your grandchild will discover how he or she is part of the divine plan of love, and that by sharing in the Eucharist he is strengthened to love God, his/her family and the whole world. You and your grandchild are caught up in this mystery. Enjoy this time of preparation together, and enjoy the life-giving fruits of the Eucharist.

Notes for the First Holy Communion Day

I Belong

for Parents and Carers of Children with Learning Difficulties

Additional notes for parents, carers and supporters of children with learning difficulties who are following "I Belong" or using "I Belong Special".

Dear Supporter

We hope that this programme can be comfortable to use with children of a variety of abilities, and that all children, no matter what their abilities, can feel they have a place in the Community of the Church.

I Belong is based very much on everyday experience and sets out to encourage you and the child you are supporting to find the deeper realities behind everyday experiences such as eating, working, making up after a row and so on. Children of all abilities are encouraged to take part and to ask questions. You will have the support of the catechist for any difficult questions you may be faced with. Children have many questions about themselves, their abilities, disabilities and things they have survived.

The themes unfold naturally during the celebration of the Eucharist and through looking at the Bible. The programme looks through everyday life at aspects of God's mercy, glory and parenthood. We understand that for some of the children, God as parent can be a difficult concept, even painful.
The programme emphasises God as a LOVING parent – a true parent who loves without conditions.

Communication
This is a very important time for the child and if possible the whole family should be involved. Meet regularly if you can. You will receive practical details but also the opportunity to meet others on the programme and be welcomed as part of the Church community.

The Bishops of England and Wales have published a booklet called "Valuing Difference" in which they welcome the contribution that disabled people can make to the Church community. It is recognised that all people are part of the Eucharistic Community. People of all abilities have a place and a role that God calls them to. "People with disabilities will be encouraged to share fully in the sacramental life. The emphasis will be on welcoming and enabling participation. The sacraments are for all; they are part of the life of faith for all." (page 38)

Your Own Spiritual Life
Of course knowledge is necessary, and it is important to know what the Bible and the Church are saying to us. Reading the Bible prayerfully is very important and the documents of Vatican II and the Catechism can also give you more information.

Don't worry if you feel you do not know much or you have forgotten a great deal. Just remember to pray together. Try very hard to put aside a certain amount of time each day, ten or fifteen minutes at least to look at the books and the Bible and say some prayers together.

Don't forget to ask for whatever help you need. The Bishops have said of children with disabilities and their families in particular, "They should have first call on parish time and energy." (page 39).

Each session the children will be exploring a theme connected with the Eucharist (Mass). They will start by looking at their ordinary experiences of the theme — beginning with **Names** *and* **Relationships** *— and then go on to think about the theme in Scripture, and in Church. Finally, they will look again at everyday experiences, and hopefully discover how the Eucharist is about* **REAL LIFE**.

Sessions can be adapted and tailored to each child's abilities, so please encourage the child you are supporting to get as much as possible from the sessions.
You can tell the catechist what things you think may help your child get the most from the sessions.
I Belong (Parents book and Child's book) are also available in braille or on tape.

SESSION 1 IN THE NAME OF THE FATHER

Preparation for First Holy Communion

Page 3 Everyday Life

The names we are called and the labels that are put on us can affect us deeply. Parents can spend a long time choosing a name for a child. It has to be just right. You may also remember that cruel name calling from parents or friends can leave a lasting impression. Negative names can make us feel that we cannot do things, but positive names help us feel that we can achieve. We recognise that everyone has some value and ability.

Pages 4 to 7 Scripture

In Scripture the use of names is often very significant. Adam, (the name means of 'the earth') represents all of us, men, women and children of all abilities. All creation is glorious. Genesis tells us that God saw creation was good…good…very good. When Adam named the animals he was accepting the responsibility he had for them. The responsibility we all have to take care of God's world..

At the Annunciation God became part of this glorious creation, thus making it even more magnificent. By becoming human, God became subject to other human beings, and was also *named*. The name Jesus (Joshua) means *saviour*. In the *Old Testament*, Joshua was one who led the Israelites over the River Jordan into the freedom of the Promised Land after their forty years in the desert. It was not by accident that Jesus was baptised in the Jordan. He is the true Joshua, leading us all to fulfilment and life.

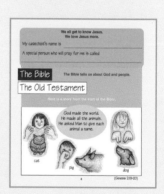

The baptism of Jesus also has links with the story of creation. Just as in *Genesis* the Spirit of God hovered over the waters of chaos and brought forth life, so the Spirit hovered over Jesus. Jesus is the *second Adam* – the new creation. In Adam, we walk in friendship with God. In Jesus, we are re-created as children of God.

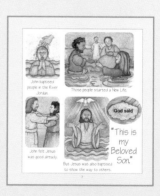

Page 8 Task

There is a picture for your child to colour in, but if they find this unhelpful, there are other tasks you can do together. Why not do a bit of washing up together.

- Dirty cups go into the water and come out clean to be used again.
- Playing with water and naming the plastic toys can be done.
- For children who use Sign language or Makaton why not make up a Sign Name?

Page 9 Church

For Jesus, his baptism was a powerful sign of his role as God's son. He knew God as a loving Father, and this helped him to do the things God asked of him. In Baptism we are all given the chance to know God as a loving father – a father who loves us all the time and will never leave us, or tell us we are not good enough, or hurt us. Baptism is the Spirit breathing life into the chaos, it is crossing over the waters of Jordan into a new life of liberty, it is God calling us to be his beloved children.

By encouraging the children to see how much God loves them we must remember that he wants the best for us and offers us choices. He will be there if we want him, no matter what has happened to us.

Page 10 Everyday Life

It would be wonderful to be constantly aware of our dignity as children of God. So often we put ourselves down, *"Oh I'm so stupid," "Oh you are a nuisance".* Perhaps we could say nice things about ourselves and others. We are all God's beloved children, and we all have dignity and worth.

At home you might go through the Our Father, explaining some of the difficult words or going through the Signs for the prayer. It is important to try and find some time to pray together. Try and find ten minutes to be quiet together and spend that time with prayers. It does not have to be just words. If the child you are supporting is a child who has little or no spoken language or who finds language difficult, try using music and sound. Use a special smell such as rose oil to be the prayer smell. Choose a sound for God's love – a rainstick perhaps.

Try and keep the same smell or sound for each prayer time so that your child begins to see that as part of the prayer. Music is a great way to bring prayer alive for children. Enjoy yourselves making a noise for God.

LORD HAVE MERCY

In this session the children will be thinking about mercy in everyday life, scripture and church. Hopefully they will come to a better understanding of the mercy of God, and how we are called to be merciful in our daily dealings with people. At the Eucharist we come before our loving God to receive infinite mercy, and are challenged and empowered to pass on this gift so freely.

Page 14 Everyday Life

Children are dependent on the merciful love of adults. Their concept of mercy will depend on what they have experienced at the hands of adults in their lives. God is traditionally portrayed as a loving parent. But we know that a child will get an idea of how God behaves as a parent from the experience of parenting they have received. Allow your child to ask questions. You may be working with a child who has not felt safe in a parent's love, or who has been bereaved. Remember to point out the constancy of God's love. Help them to feel loved and accepted, by taking their questions seriously. All of this is part of a healing process which also helps bring us closer to God. We also recognise that many of the adults who support the children may themselves have negative parenting experiences and find God as Father a difficult concept. Please always ask for support from your catechist and priest should you need it.

Page 16 Old Testament

The creation stories of the Old Testament.

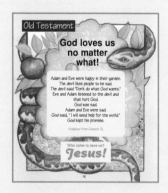

We know from the story of creation and Adam and Eve that God did not intend there to be any suffering in his world. When sin came into the world it made things less than perfect.

In the past people have felt that you must deserve it if you have a problem or a disability, but we know this is not true. God asks us to offer to him the things that hurt us, so that he can help us.

Page 17 New Testament

We will be looking closely at the story of the Prodigal Son. This is a wonderful story to make into a simple play or puppet show that the children can take part in. They love the chance to give advice to each character. It gives them a chance to explore doing things wrong and both receiving and giving forgiveness. Children who have had difficult experiences can find a way of checking with God — the loving and forgiving Father — whether he really loves them.

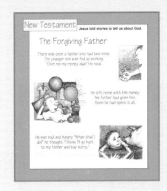

Page 19 Picture to colour in

You may find that using the puppet show is a better way of exploring this story with your child, if they find colouring in difficult.

Page 20/21 Church

The Sign for Mercy is both hands gently stroking down. The word Eleison (in Kyrie Eleison — Lord have mercy) is a Greek word thought to come from the word for olive. This is from the symbol of the olive branch that the dove gave to Noah when the flood was over.

With your child you can explore how mercy and forgiveness are linked. The Prodigal Son came back to his father and said sorry.

"The quality of mercy is not strained; It droppeth as the gentle rain from heaven upon the place beneath. It is twice blest: it blesseth him that gives and him that takes.
'Tis mightiest in the mightiest; it becomes the throned
monarch better than his crown; …
It is enthroned in the hearts of kings,
It is an attribute of God himself…"
Merchant of Venice, Act IV

SESSION 3 CELEBRATING OUR RESCUE

This is the first of two sessions to help the children prepare for their First Reconciliation. At the next session they will be thinking about how God helps them "get it right" and how Reconciliation can give us help for the future. To begin with though, they will be thinking of how we are always being rescued by God. Reconciliation is always taking place in everyday life, and the Sacrament of Reconciliation is an opportunity to praise God for his understanding, help and forgiveness in the past.

Page 25 Everyday Life

You could remind your child of any rescue they have seen. Maybe a road accident or fire. Perhaps they tried to rescue a bird fallen out of a tree, or stood up for a younger child when they were being bullied. If your child has ever been lost, you could discuss how they felt. (The odds are **YOU** were even more worried than they were! Use this as an illustration of how pleased God is when we are back on the right path.)

What we need to get across to the children is that they are basically GOOD and that sometimes just like everyone they lose their way and need rescuing, not that they are more sinful than everyone else and need constant correcting to be occasionally good and lovable. We only have to ask and God will rescue us.

Page 27 Old Testament

Many people have a distorted picture of God because of their own life experiences. They may feel that they have done something really bad and that God is punishing them, or that if their faith was strong enough God would not allow their life to be so difficult. It feels then that God is very far away. We need to get back to the image of God as a loving parent who loves us and wants what is best for us. God is Emmanuel – God with us.

"Can a mother forget her child?…(Isaiah 49.15

Page 28 New Testament

The Parable of the Lost Sheep is one of three parables – (the Lost Sheep, the Lost Coin, the Prodigal Son) all together in Luke's Gospel – about God's joy over returning sinners. They are three stories told to the self-righteous scribes and Pharisees who were disgusted at Jesus because he mixed with "publicans and sinners". In Jewish law, certain occupations automatically made people sinners, as you were unable to keep the outward observances of the law.

There were also rules in the Old Law that said people were unclean or in some ways unacceptable if they had certain illnesses or diseases. Jesus and his friends however, showed that all people are acceptable and lovable to God.

Page 29 Picture to colour

Page 30 Everyday life again

The children will be helped to think about their feelings, and how they are useful signals to their needs. When you care for a child you need to empathise with their feelings of anger, hurt, envy, etc. and help them find appropriate and constructive ways of handling their problems. This can often be very difficult and you will undoubtedly need to spend time in prayer asking God to give you a helping hand. Never say *"I will not love you/ like you if…"* Apart from being a devastating statement, it is not a true reflection of God's parenthood. **GOD IS LOVE.**

Page 31 Church

Because Catholics have often inherited this tendency to stress the distance between God and us, reconciliation is seen as something very negative. Try to stress the **celebration** aspect with your child. We are celebrating God's forgiving love and on-going help. A modern definition of a sacrament is *"a festive action in which Christians assemble to celebrate their lived experience and to call to heart their common story. The action is a symbol of God's care for us in Christ. Enacting the symbol brings us closer to one another in the church, and to the Lord who is there for us."*

Tad Guzie. The Book of Sacramental Basics.

You may be caring for a child who is suffering from guilt feelings over events that they had no control over in their life. They may have given way to these feelings of confusion and made mistakes. Support them as they try and make sense of the things that have happened to them and remember that Reconciliation is there as a great help in being rescued from confusion as well as sin.

SESSION 4 GOD HELPS ME GET IT RIGHT

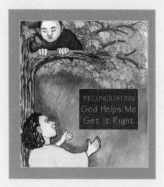

At our last session we thought about how God rescues us from past failings, and how reconciliation is going on in life all the time. We go to Reconciliation to CELEBRATE God's forgiving love. This session we are still thinking about celebrating, but with a focus on the future. When we CONFIDE in the priest we are CONFIDENT that the sacrament gives us help for the times we "get it wrong".

Page 37-38 Everyday Life

Remind the children about the achievements they have made. All children, no matter what their abilities, are good at something. One child I know who is very disabled has the most beautiful smile – and uses it to full effect! You can offer lots of help and encouragement in the things they do. Each child has their own gifts and abilities and therefore there is no need to compare one with another. Show interest and you will find a child blossoms under your care. God is a good parent who holds out a helping hand. God's belief in us gives us the courage to believe in ourselves. God says, "Go on I know you can do it," and we find it is true.

Page 39-40 New Testament

The children have had two parables about forgiveness already — The Prodigal Son and the Lost Sheep. Each story ends with a party – a celebration that what was lost is now found. They are now hearing about a real-life situation when Jesus **"practises what he preaches"**. Jesus searches out the lost son of Abraham and the celebration itself brings about the wonderful transformation in Zacchaeus.

Zacchaeus, the tax collector, was a collaborator with the Roman authorities, so was considered a traitor by the 'decent' people. Tax collectors collected the money that the Romans exacted, but they were allowed to collect any amount they liked and they pocketed the difference. It was this man whom Jesus singled out to dine with. The effect on Zacchaeus was remarkable. Having been affirmed by Jesus, he confessed his guilt and decided to make amends. His offer to pay back four times what he had wrongly taken was a direct reference to the Jewish law – he was acting as a good Jew now not as a public sinner, for as Jesus said of him, *"This man too is a son of Abraham."* The message for us is — **if we treat our children as sons and daughters of God they will act like sons and daughters of God.**

Page 41 Picture to Colour in

There is a song called *Come Down Zacchaeus* which the children might like to learn. Ask at your church or local school for a copy.

Page 42 The Sacrament

Reconciliation can be difficult to understand. You may need to spend time playing with your child, finding words or signs that fit the idea of being rescued and reconciling with God and with each other. Emphasise that all of us are made in God's image, and that is not a physical image but a spiritual one. A person with a disability is equally made in God's image as someone considered to be not disabled. God really does believe in us and love us. He says to us as he did to the woman taken in adultery, *"Go and sin no more"*.

Finally — enjoy your child's First Reconciliation. It is a celebration, just as Baptism, Confirmation, First Communion, Marriage, Ordination, and even the Sacrament of the Sick are celebrations.

SESSION 5 GLORY TO GOD IN THE HIGHEST

This session the children will be thinking about glory. This is a difficult concept, but a very important one. Everything Jesus did was for the GLORY of his Father, and to follow in his footsteps all our actions should also be for the honour and glory of God.

Page 49 *Everyday Life*

The children may not have had many experiences of actually receiving GLORY, but they may well have had experiences which leave them gasping with wonder. A magnificent fireworks display, or the first time they see snow are two possibilities among thousands.

Page 51 *Old Testament*

The **GLORY** (*shekinah*) of God is spoken of again and again in the Old Testament. In the burning bush episode we learn that we cannot name God (*I Am who I Am*) for God is beyond us.

However we learn that this **HOLY GOD** is a God who **SAVES**. God led the slaves through the desert to freedom, the *shekinah* remaining with them as a pillar of fire by night, and of cloud by day.

Page 52-53 *New Testament*

God chooses people to do various tasks with him. He chose Moses to be one of the greatest prophets of the Bible, even though Moses was worried because he couldn't speak properly.

God then chose the Shepherds outside Bethlehem to be the first to see the Holy Family when Jesus was born. The shepherds could not follow the strict rules about washing set by the Pharisees and so were thought of as less than good people.

God often chooses people that the rest of the world might not think of as important and shares his **GLORY** with them.

Once again he approaches people caught up in slavery, and gives them the Good News of peace. God is with us — Emmanuel.

Page 54 Picture to colour in

It might not be the right time of year, but if your child prefers why not get out the nativity set and talk about how Jesus was born. Perhaps your child would like to make a little present for Jesus. It can be something your child is good at. Give Jesus a smile for example.

Page 55 Church

The whole of the Eucharist is a prayer of praise and thanks to the **GLORY of God**. (The word *Eucharist* means thank you. In Greece today you can still hear people saying *efcharisto* — thank you).

At the Eucharist try and help your child be aware of how much we offer God praise and Glory. In their session the children will be thinking about the **GLORIA**, but there are other important prayers of praise. The words of the preface change according to what aspect of God's glory we are praising, and being thankful for. There is also the beautiful prayer,

> *Through him, with him and in him,*
> *In the unity of the Holy Spirit,*
> *all glory and honour is yours,*
> *almighty Father,*
> *for ever and ever.*

The response of **AMEN** is for everyone to take part in the prayer. The children can shout it out or Sign it or wave a large flag. Help your child to be as involved as possible.

When the shepherds left the magnificent glory of God on the hillside, they arrived at the quiet glory of a baby in a manger. At the Eucharist we meet the quiet glory of God under the sign of the consecrated bread and wine. The more we are aware of the wonder of the **REAL PRESENCE** the more will our children appreciate this breath-taking **MYSTERY OF FAITH.**

Page 56 Everyday Life

Through Jesus the glory of God can shine brightly in each one of us. We are a holy people, each of us like the burning bush if we choose to be. When we approach one another we approach holy ground. Let us teach our children to reverence the holiness of others, and we can do this through how we love our children. To love God and to love our neighbour are two sides of the same coin.

SESSION 6 — THIS IS THE WORD OF THE LORD

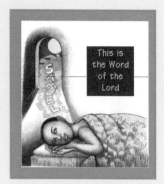

In this session the children will be thinking about LISTENING to the word of God. Listening is about opening your heart to what God wants to say to you. All children can learn to listen in this way through spending time quietly each day with Jesus.

The first half of the Eucharist is called the Liturgy of the Word where we can focus on the reason for glorifying God.

Page 61 Everyday Life

Here the children look at different ways we can **LISTEN**. Knowing that many children have difficulties in concentrating or in hearing, the children can explore how we listen in different ways and take notice of what is around us.

In this way we can explore how God speaks to us in different ways, and how we can **LISTEN** to him. We listen with our eyes, ears, through touch and our hearts.

Maybe you could look for the different things around that are used to get our attention or tell us things; road signs, posters, lights, etc.

Page 63

The children read the story of Samuel in the temple. Hannah had wept and prayed for a child, and promised him to the Lord if she should have one. When Samuel was born, Hannah sang a song of praise to God, recounting the marvellous saving works of God in lifting up the poor and feeding the hungry. Years later, Mary would use this song as a basis for her song of praise to God, when her cousin Elizabeth acknowledged the presence of the Saviour in Mary's womb. This prayer, known as the **Magnificat**, is still used every evening in the *Prayer of the Church (Divine Office)*.

The children will concentrate on the story of Samuel who listened to God. The children are like Samuel (and Jesus) in that they are gifts from God. Baptism, not only marks their entry into the community, but also makes them prophets who listen to God's word, hold it in their hearts and carry it out to others through how they live — just as Samuel and Jesus did. Holy Communion is a way of listening and receiving Jesus into their hearts, and so becoming a full member of the community.

Page 65 New Testament

In the Old Testament, there were many prophets who brought God's word to the people. Jesus is more than the greatest of the prophets – he **IS** God's Word. Jesus is the *embodiment* of God. God responds to our poverty and need by becoming poor and needy. God is indeed *Emmanuel — "God with us"*.

The word *"Bethlehem"* means "House of Bread". In Jesus the songs of Hannah and Mary are fulfilled, for in him God comes to our rescue – the poor and hungry are fed.

The promise is kept today in the Eucharist when God is with us as the Bread of Life, and we go out from the Eucharist with a mission to feed the hungry – to be saviours ourselves to those in need.

This is an opportunity to get to know Jesus. Perhaps you could share a family meal together where the food has to be shared out – rather than ready plated – and the children must help share it.

Page 66 Picture to colour in

Page 67 Church

The readings at the Eucharist can be difficult to understand and children can get bored. It can be even more boring if your child cannot hear what is said, or cannot see what is happening. You can discuss with your parish priest having a Eucharist with the children that includes *Sign Language*, or you could take activities using the Eucharist with you to church.

Those who can, could listen out for certain words such as Glory or Father.

Put together a church bag which includes pens, paper and textures that you could use during the Mass to help your child with different parts of it.

Page 68 Everyday Life

The children are finishing with a Snakes and Ladders type game, where they go up a Ladder if they listen to good/nice things, and down a Snake if they don't listen (or listen to bad ideas!) Please play it at home with your children. It is giving them the message that what we listen to affects us.

SESSION 7   BREAD TO OFFER

Until now the children were thinking about the first part of the Eucharist — the Liturgy of the Word. They are now turning to the second part — the Liturgy of the Eucharist. In this session the children will be thinking about the Preparation of the Gifts/Offertory.

Page 73 Everyday Life

Try and spend time with your child talking about where food comes from. Perhaps you could show them or work with them in preparing a meal.

You could look at where some of the food comes from. Do you have a *Traidcraft* or *Tearfund* stall at your church?

But don't forget that the bread of the Eucharist is not just about food but about sacrifice. Many people have to give up a great deal to feed their children. Jesus gave his life – his body and blood – to feed us.

Take this slowly with your child. It can be very difficult to understand.

Page 75 Old Testament

The people in the desert were entirely at the mercy of God (and the heat, lack of food and water, etc.) In their wanderings they learnt to trust that God would provide, and developed a real understanding of what *"bread"* stands for. To a large extent we have lost this understanding, and maybe even lost a realisation of how dependent we are on God. When hardships hit us we can either grumble, like the Israelites did at first, or develop an attitude of trust in God, who **"gives us our daily bread"**.

The lsraelites were instructed to gather only enough for their daily needs. If they gathered too much the manna putrefied. However the day before the Sabbath they were instructed to gather twice as much so they could rest on the Sabbath. This amount did not putrefy and they were able to eat on the day of rest. Throughout their journey the Israelites were fed on the manna, rather like we, the new People of God, are fed on the bread of life throughout our life's journey.   (*Exodus 16*)

Children who cannot eat, know what it is to rely on others for all the food they receive.

Page 76 New Testament

Three of the gospels, Matthew, Mark and Luke, give accounts of the Last Supper of Jesus. John does not. Instead, he puts his teaching about the Eucharist in Chapter 6, the Feeding of the Five Thousand. The children will be thinking about the little boy who offered up his five loaves and two fishes. Jesus took these, and enabled his disciples to feed the crowd, with twelve baskets of scraps left over. As adults, we can go deeper into the mystery, and read all that Jesus said about himself after this great **sign**. One thing worth mentioning is that Jesus said, *"I am the Bread of Life."* He makes seven **"I AM"** statements in John's gospel. You may remember that when Moses asked God's name he was told **"I AM WHO I AM."** Jesus is telling us that he, God, the great I AM, is feeding us with his own self, and we shall live forever.

Page 78 Picture to colour in

Page 79 Church

As said earlier, we are probably out of touch with the deep significance of presenting bread to God. We are so dependent on food that we are offering God our very existence. To put it less grandly, when we offer up the bread it stands for all the sweat and labour, the tedium of the past week – everything we do to keep a roof above our heads and the wolf from the door. The offering of the money is also deeply significant. It is not an interruption of the Eucharist, but very much part of it. At the beginning of the Bible, in Genesis 14, Melchisedech, the king of Salem and Priest of God Most High, offered bread and wine to God, and Abram (later called Abraham) gave him a tenth of all his wealth. We will think about the wine next time.

Page 80 Everyday life

Just as the disciples fed the crowds with the bread, we go out to others to feed the world. We all have gifts from God no matter who we are or how others have thought of us. Our gratitude to God opens up a spirit of generosity in us, and the Eucharist not only feeds us but empowers us to go out to others.

Some children may feel that they have a disability or other reason why they feel they have nothing much to offer others. Encourage them to think of all the things they offer without realising.

A wonderful story is the story of *Blessed Margaret of Castello* – blind and physically disabled she was abandoned by her parents as useless, but proved to be a great help to many people and spent her life caring for others.

FRUIT OF THE VINE

In this session the children will be thinking about the wine which we use at the Eucharist, and why we use it. As adults we can understand that wine not only symbolises celebration, but that it also stands for sorrow — we talk of a cup of sorrow. If we share a cup with someone we are intimately connected with them. We share their destiny. Although the children will touch on the sorrowful aspect, they will be concentrating on the joy of celebrations.

Page 85 *Everyday Life*

Often children don't like the taste of wine so they will be thinking of the tastes they didn't like when they were younger, but do now. Even children fed through a tube can often taste the feeds and have flavours they either like or really dislike. If your child is fed through a tube either naso-gastrically or by gastrostomy you could look at nice and nasty smells with them as smell and taste often go together.

At home you might like the children to have a taste of wine if they haven't yet done so. Communion wine is usually sweet and rich.

Page 87 *Old Testament*

The Passover feast was held every spring to celebrate the deliverance from slavery of the People of God. The feast was not just held in memory of the past. To the Jews, celebrating this feast makes God's saving action present and available to them in the here and now.

The People of God thought of themselves as the vineyard of God. Other references to themselves as God's vineyard are in Psalm 80 – *"You have brought a grapevine out of Egypt ... Turn to us Almighty God ... Come and save this grapevine that you planted"*.

Choose a simple song to include in this session. Children with autism or other language difficulties often enjoy music and can join in with percussion instruments. Why not make one of your own with dried peas in a jar to shake?

Page 89 *New Testament*

The children will think about the celebration that Jesus provided. So many gallons of wine is really lavish – rather like the miracle of the loaves and fishes when twelve baskets were left over! The abundance of wine is a symbol that the fullness of the Kingdom has arrived (Isaiah 25:6). It was *"on the third day"* Jesus took the water, standing for the old ritualism of the original Covenant, and changed it into wine, standing for the wine of the New Covenant.

Page 91 Picture to colour in

If your child finds the picture too difficult to fill in you could make some simple prints using poster paints and potatoes.

- *Cut a potato in half and carve out a simple shape such as a cup or flower for the wedding and print them on a piece of paper.*
- *Children with visual impairment or who are blind might like to make a collage using different textures – satins for the bride and corrugated card or other textures for cups and water jars.*
- *Plasticine models are also a great way for children to explore the story of the wedding at Cana.*

Page 92 Church

The link between the Jewish Passover and the Eucharist is very obvious in the Passover prayer (on page 87 in the children's book). The Eucharist is very much a Thank You prayer for all the good things of creation.

We also think of ourselves as a vine. Jesus said he was the vine and we are the branches. He is not separate from us – a vine IS the branches – we are the New Risen Body of Christ. **"Whatever you do to the least one of these, you do it to me,"** said Jesus.

Just as the Passover makes God's action present for the Jews, so the Eucharist makes God's action present for us. We are liberated from slavery to sin by receiving the life of Christ. We not only look to the past, to Christ's redeeming acts of death and resurrection, but also to the future. At the Last Supper Jesus said he would not drink again till he drank the new wine of the Kingdom of God. At the Eucharist we bring about the Wedding Feast of the Lamb, and God eats with the New People of God.

Page 93 and 94 Everyday Life

The Kingdom of God will not come about unless we take the Eucharist seriously. Properly understood, the Eucharist means that we join with Jesus in bringing the Good News to the world no matter what the cost.

In the Eucharist we are uniting ourselves to the selfless love of Jesus in giving up his life for his friends. *"No one has greater love than he who gives up his life for his friends."* (John 15:13) This is exactly what Jesus did.

SESSION 9 DO THIS IN MEMORY OF ME

*We now come to the heart of the Eucharist — the "Institution Narrative". At this part of the Eucharist the Holy Spirit is invoked: "Let your Spirit come upon these gifts," and the **Words of Consecration** are said. Jesus is made present on the altar in a new way. His presence remains in the consecrated hosts reserved in the tabernacle on the altar. The word tabernacle comes from the tent of meeting in the desert (Exodus 25:8). He is already present as God, in Scripture, in the priest and people, and other ways, but this new presence is so special it is called the **Real Presence**. In this sacrament Christ is present in a unique way, whole and entire, God and man, substantially and permanently.*

Page 99 Everyday Life

We have meals for all sorts of reasons and in many different forms. Even if we cannot eat the same food together we can gather together at a meal time and share ideas and thoughts, catching up on the day's events.

Page 101 Old Testament

There is only one on the Old Testament in this session, as we are concentrating more on the Last Supper, and we have talked about the Passover before. However it might be worth noting that the word Passover comes from the fact that the Israelites sacrificed a lamb, and put the blood on their door-posts so that God **"passed over"** their houses. Because of the blood of the lamb the Israelites did not suffer the tenth plague – the death of the eldest son. (We are not covering this with the children).

Page 102 New Testament

Jesus took an existing feast, the most important of the Jewish celebrations, and changed it into something new. Throughout the Old Testament, God is constantly renewing the Covenant made with human beings. In the Book of Jeremiah, God promises a New Covenant, not like the previous one. In the New Covenant, *"I will put my law within them. I will write it upon their hearts. I will be their God and they shall be my people ... They shall all know me, from the least of them to the greatest. I will forgive them and forget their sins."* (Jeremiah 31:31-34)

Jesus brought about this New Covenant at his Last Supper

when he, the new Lamb of God, offered his life, present in the bread and in the Cup of Salvation (*the Blood of the New and Everlasting Covenant*).

Once again, we are not mentioning 'blood' to the children, although we are talking about Jesus dying for us. In Western cultures, we usually associate *blood* with *death*; for the Jews, *blood* meant *life*.

Talking about blood can be difficult in Western cultures where it is often about death, but we can talk about how our blood going through our hearts and all through our body keeps us alive. People give their blood – just a part of it to help save another person's life. Perhaps your child has received blood or something made from donated blood to help keep your child alive and healthy.

Jesus gave all his blood to keep us all alive and healthy for God.

Page 104 Picture to colour in

If you like making bread, this is a good time to make some. Children who might not be able to colour the picture will love the feel of the dough and the wonderful smell of it baking.

My children enjoyed decorating biscuits with the faces of the disciples at the Last Supper and then sharing them out. Remember you can use textures here too with hundreds and thousands and little icing balls. *Have some fun!*

Page 105 Church

If you can, help your child to listen out for the words of the Consecration. If you think this will be difficult, take along some pictures to church and help your child see what is happening.

For deaf/blind children you will need textures and small activities to help the children know each part of the Eucharist. Build up a Mass box with cues that your child learns as they get used to each part of the Mass.

This idea can be used with children with a variety of abilities, particularly those who have problems with concentration.

Page 106 Everyday Life

Enjoy meals together. Even if your child cannot eat the food perhaps because of being tube fed, they are still part of your family. Enjoy all the time together.

SESSION 10 BODY OF CHRIST

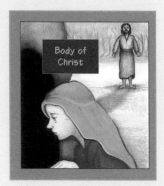

This session we are looking at the words the priest says as he distributes the host and the cup — "The Body of Christ" and "The Blood of Christ". We are thinking about HOW Christ is present in the bread and wine.

Page 111 Everyday Life

The children will be thinking about how tadpoles and caterpillars change into frogs and butterflies. The outer appearances change, but the inner reality is the same. They will be led to think about how the opposite happens at the Eucharist. At Mass the outer appearances of the bread and wine are the same, but the inner reality is different.

Old Testament

There is no Old Testament story this session in order to have two New Testament stories. The Old Testament stories have been leading up to this fulfilment of God's promise in the New Covenant.

Pages 113 to116 New Testament

The two stories (Christ appearing to Mary Magdalen and to the friends on the way to Emmaus) have been used to illustrate that he looked different. He had a different kind of body…

These are especially joyful stories and full of hope for all our futures. You may find this is a difficult part of the course if your child has an illness which may shorten his or her life. Do not be afraid to ask for support from those you trust should your child use this as an opportunity to talk about death and the promised afterlife.

Children who have been recently bereaved may also ask questions. Adults in Western cultures seem to find death a difficult subject. In my experience children are quite happy to ask all sorts of questions.

Page 115 Picture to colour in

Try planting some mustard and cress. At first it will look as though there isn't much life to be seen, but soon you will see shoots and tiny leaves.

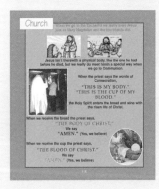

Page 118 Church

It is in the Eucharist that we recognise him too. We look at the outward appearances of bread and wine, but recognise Jesus in the **"breaking of the bread"**. Don't try to go into long explanations of how Christ is present. It is such a unique mystery it is called **THE Mystery of Faith**. Technical explanations might take away the wonder of it all, rather like explaining how rainbows occur at the very moment the child has been surprised by one. The introduction about tadpoles and caterpillars is more about the wonder of the changes that they can see, to prepare them for the wonder of the change that they can't see.

Page 119 Everyday life

There is so much to say, and so little time! When we go to the Eucharist sometimes we feel wonderful, sometimes we feel hypocritical, sometimes we feel we have the strength to conquer the world afterwards, sometimes we go back to old bad habits. The truth of it is that we are a wounded people just as Jesus was wounded. If we could try to look at one another in the community and indeed in the world, and see this new Body of Christ, and love one another with the compassion of Christ, the Eucharist will have borne fruit. There will be more about this aspect of the Eucharist in the next session, but for this one, in the last week or so before your child's communion, encourage them to pray quietly to Jesus, and pray together as a family if you feel you can do so. Bearing in mind that they may not feel anything very much after their First Holy Communion (there's a lot of practicalities for them to think about, and they might be nervous), tell them that the time after receiving the Eucharist is a very special time, both for them and Jesus. Time spent in stillness and reverence will help them *"recognise him in the breaking of the bread.'*

Take your child to church as often as you can to be part of the community. *"The unity of the Church is not complete if people with disabilities are not included and participating fully when their community celebrates and receives the Eucharist."* *(Valuing Difference* page 41)

This can be a difficult time for parents and carers who have avoided taking their disabled children to church for fear that they would cause a nuisance or disturbance, or because there is no interpreter available. However the Bishops have recognised that *"People with disabilities will express their faith in Christ's presence in the Eucharist in different ways."* (Page 42).

SESSION 11 TO LOVE AND TO SERVE

Our last session of the programme! This will be a shorter session than the earlier ones to allow time for a party at the end. Please encourage your child to finish their book at home. We will be concentrating on getting the children to write a "thank you letter" to their Prayer Sponsors. Some of you may have already asked your children to do this. Your child will also be given the name of a new child for them to pray for next year.

Page 123 Everyday Life

At meal times you could make the link between everyday food and spiritual food. Communion gives us strength for living as Christians. If we don't eat of this food regularly we are (literally) not in communion with the Body of Christ. The Eucharist is called the **"source and summit"** of the People of God.

If you don't normally thank God for your food at meal times you might like to introduce this, and add a prayer for those who haven't enough to eat.

Page 125 Old Testament

Use the pictures as a reminder and cue to all the stories in the Bible that lead us to Jesus.

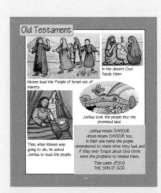

Page 126 New Testament

This story, like the one of Emmaus last session, is a **"model"** of the Eucharist. Christ feeds us and asks us to do likewise: *"Feed my lambs and sheep"*. Note that the apostles, including trained fishermen, couldn't catch fish themselves. There are many other stories you could tell your children about how we bring about the Kingdom of God (how we enter the Promised Land). For example: *"I was hungry and you gave me food"* is a good one. *(Matthew 25:34-40)*

Use a song to help the children understand how Jesus felt and get them to remember that Jesus forgave Peter and Peter agreed to carry on and build the Church, because he did love Jesus.

Page 128 *Picture to colour in*

Again this is a chance to use other materials and textures for children who find colouring in less important.

From a practical point they could make a small model with clay or plasticine for a friend they have fallen out with, just as Jesus made breakfast for Peter that morning on the beach, even though Peter had denied him, only a few days before.

Page 129 *Church*

Sometimes people say they don't need to go to church as they are just as good as church-goers, or even that church-goers are hypocrites. But the Eucharist, properly understood, strengthens us to serve others. What we put into it, and what we receive from it has a direct bearing on how we live every day.

Sometimes there are special Events or Masses aimed specifically at people with particular disabilities. They are open to all to attend and can be wonderful experiences for all. Don't be tempted to only take your child to church during these special times. *"The provision of such a liturgy (no matter how frequently) is not a reason for failing to make appropriate provision to enable people with particular disabilities to play a full and proper part in regular parish liturgy."* (*Valuing Difference page 37*)

As the child's parent or supporter you may need to take on the role as advocate in this matter as well. Ask your parish priest if there is a Diocesan Special Needs Adviser and how you can get in touch.

Your child has prepared for the Eucharist, and received Holy Communion. The catechists hope that the children, and you, have all enjoyed the Course. There is so much to learn, and we will never understand the glory of the Eucharist in this life. However, we cannot know God by the intellect. It is the heart that understands and loves. May God bless you and your family.

Dear Carer,

Your child, foster child, grandchild, friend's child is preparing for his/her First Communion. You may have all come along a difficult road to this process. You may have found that at first your child was not ready alongside people of his/her own age to receive these Sacraments. This can be very painful for a family who wishes to see their children all received into the full life of the Church.

In Valuing Difference it is stated clearly "if it is determined that a parishioner who is disabled is not yet ready to receive the Eucharist, great care is taken in explaining the reasons for this decision. In such cases it is vital that the individual and the family or caring group are given opportunities to talk about this decision and to explore how to move forward." (page 43).

You may find that people within the Church are not as aware of the issues around disability as you would wish. Have patience with people who may not have had the opportunity to live and work with disabled people the way you have. Most people will be caring, even if they are clumsy about it. Take the opportunity to get people to listen to you as advocate for your child, but also for them to listen to the child -through their own voice or a form of interpretation.

All of us are made in God's image whatever abilities we are given. All of us have a special value and something to offer those around us.

Spend a few moments every day with your child praying. Use the same props and cues each time so that he/she will understand that certain smells or textures and actions are about spending time with God.

 Why not put together a little prayer box? Keep a cloth with shapes such as a cross or fish sewn or glued on to it. Use pictures and smells to set the scene. Incense sticks are cheap and easy to come by these days, and can remind you of church. You will know what your child can deal with. Begin and end your prayers with the Sign of the Cross. This will help your child focus on his or her prayer.
Enjoy the time together with God.

Ref: Bishops Conference of England and Wales – Valuing Difference 1998 -
People with Disabilities in the Life and Mission of the Church – Catholic Education Service

MAKATON
Prayers

Our Father

Our Father, who art in heaven,
hallowed be thy name;

Our

Father

in heaven

name

Your kingdom come;
Your will be done

Your

kingdom

come

Your

will

be done

on earth as it is in heaven.
Give us this day our daily bread

Earth

as it is in

heaven

give us today

our daily bread

and forgive us our sins as we forgive those
who hurt us; and lead us not into temptation,

forgive us

our sins

as we forgive those who hurt us

lead us not into temptation

but deliver us from evil.

deliver

evil

Hail Mary

Hail, Mary,

Hail

Mary

M

a

r   y

full of grace,
the Lord is with you.

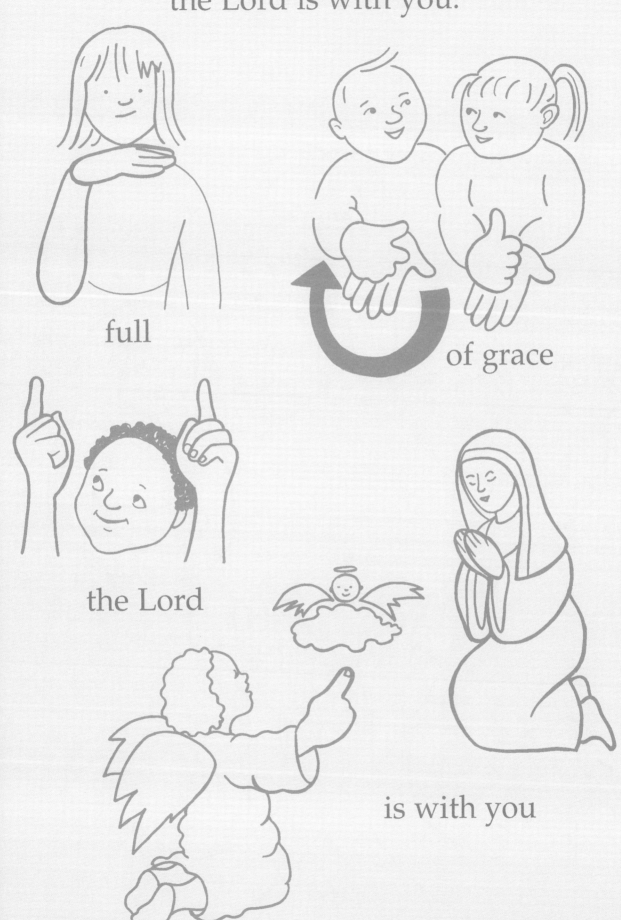

full

of grace

the Lord

is with you

Blessed are you among women,
and blessed is your baby, Jesus

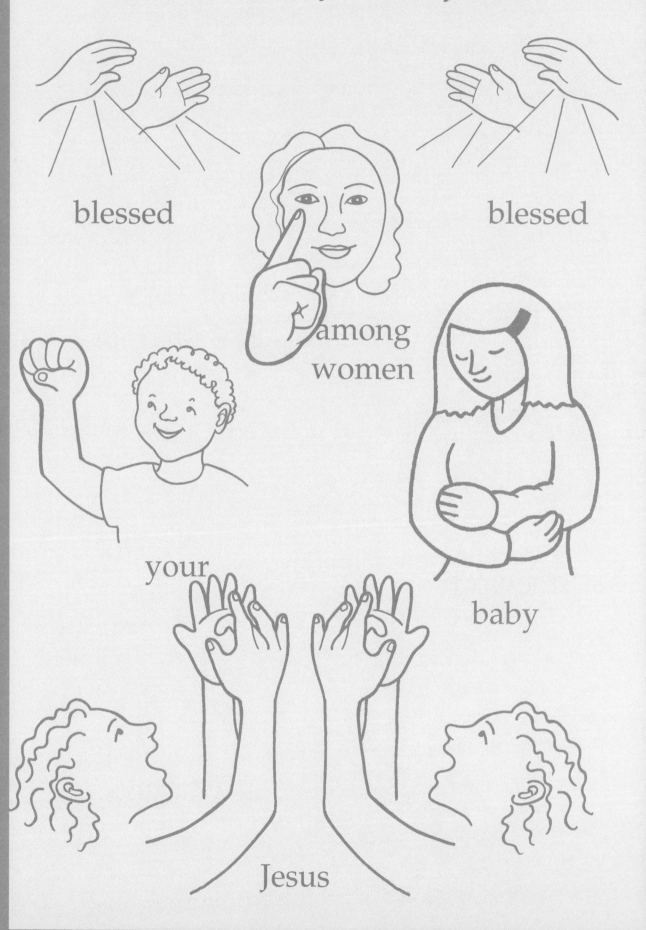

blessed

blessed

among
women

your

baby

Jesus

Holy Mary, Mother of God,

Holy

Mary

M

a

r

y

Mother

God

pray for us sinners,
now and when we die.

pray for us

sinners

now

and when we

die

Notes for the First Holy Communion Day